I CAN ONLY IMAGINE

A 4-WEEK DEVOTIONAL FOR STUDENTS

THIS BOOK BELONGS TO: Jackson Autin

DATE STARTED: 6-28-18

PUBLISHED BY YM360 AND City ON A HILL

I Can Only Imagine: A 4-Week Devotional Journal For Students

©2018 by youthministry360. All rights reserved.

Published by youthministry360 in the United States of America.

I CAN ONLY IMAGINE is a trademark of MercyMe Music, Inc. Used by permission.

ISBN 13: 9781935832690
ISBN 10: 1935832697

No part of this publication may be reproduced, stored in a retrieval system, or transmitted in any form or by any means electronic or mechanical, including photocopy, recording, or any information storage and retrieval system now known or to be invented, without prior permission in writing from the publisher.

Any reference within this piece to Internet addresses of web sites not under the administration of youthministry360 is not to be taken as an endorsement of these web sites by youthministry360; neither does youthministry360 vouch for their content.

Unless otherwise noted, Scripture quotations are from the ESV® Bible (The Holy Bible, English Standard Version®), copyright © 2001 by Crossway, a publishing ministry of Good News Publishers. Used by permission. All rights reserved.

Authors: Andy Blanks, Robbie Crawford, Jeremy Horton, Clay Wyatt
Executive Editor: Andy Blanks
Design: Laurel-Dawn Latshaw
Copy Editing: Paige Townley

TABLE OF CONTENTS

Foreword	6
Getting Started	8
Week 1 Intro	10
Day 1	12
Day 2	14
Day 3	16
Day 4	18
Day 5	20
Day 6	22
Day 7	23
Week 2 Intro	24
Day 1	26
Day 2	28
Day 3	30
Day 4	32
Day 5	34
Day 6	36
Day 7	37
Week 3 Intro	38
Day 1	40
Day 2	42
Day 3	44
Day 4	46
Day 5	48
Day 6	50
Day 7	51
Week 4 Intro	52
Day 1	54
Day 2	56
Day 3	58
Day 4	60
Day 5	62
Day 6	64
Day 7	65
Acknowledgments	68

If you've seen the movie *I Can Only Imagine*, and if you're reading this it's likely that you have, you know that the film is as much about the relationship I had with my dad as it was about me writing a song. My dad had a temper. He was abusive. When he had a bad day, he took it out on me. I went through a growth spurt in 6th grade, and after that, he never laid a finger on me. But the emotional abuse was significant. I've used the word *monster* to describe the way he was back then.

Then, during my freshmen year in high school, my dad was diagnosed with cancer. By the time he died when I was in college, he had become one of the godliest men I knew.

How?

The power of the Gospel.

I watched my dad go from being the guy you'd be afraid to cross when he walked into a room to the man I'd hear weeping while praying for my brother and me. I got to have a front row seat to the transformation God worked in my dad's life. By the time my father ultimately lost his fight with cancer, he had become a man whom I wanted to pattern my life after.

This change was remarkable in my dad. But I had to go through my own change. I remember sitting up nights with my dad while he was in bed getting one of his various medications. My dad would want to talk, but he'd have to pry answers out of me. It was like we were meeting for the first time. I remember not wanting to talk while my dad was hanging onto every word I would say, sincerely trying to make up for lost time. I was the one who was bitter.

The turning point for me was that my dad didn't give up. He kept chiseling away at my defenses. Over time, I opened up. One of the hardest things for me when dad passed away was not having him to talk to anymore.

Do you see how powerful the Gospel is? The love, redemption, forgiveness, and ultimately hope that is made possible in Jesus flies like a banner over my story. What a difference Jesus made in my life in and in the life of my father.

These same themes – love, forgiveness, redemption, and hope – are not only the driving themes of the movie and the story of my dad and me, but they are also the themes unpacked in this book. If you watched the movie, you know that spending time with God and recording those thoughts in my journal was a big part of my spiritual journey. This journal can be a big part of yours too. It's a powerful way of helping you get one-on-one with God and to really dig deep into who God is and how He is working in and through you.

My prayer is that your time spent with God while working through this book is time that God uses to change you. Much like you saw through my story, God is at work in your life. Who knows where He will lead you and what He will equip you to do? Hang in there. Don't give up. And watch to see what God is ready to show you.

Bart Millard
Lead Singer, *MercyMe*

getting started

If you're holding this book, chances are you've seen the movie *I Can Only Imagine*. If you've seen the movie, you know what a compelling story it is. God's love. Forgiveness. Redemption. Hope. All of these themes and more were woven into the story of Bart Millard and his father.

DID YOU KNOW THAT GOD DESIRES TO WEAVE THESE THEMES THROUGH THE STORY OF YOUR LIFE AS WELL?

Depending on how well you know God, you may have interacted with God in these ways already. Hopefully, you already know God's love, and if you know God's love, then you've felt the forgiveness He offers. But maybe you don't know God yet. Or perhaps you know God, but you just haven't been watching for how He's working in your life. This book is a great way to help you begin to see what God has done, is doing, and will do in your life.

One of the truths communicated in *I Can Only Imagine* is that Jesus changes everything. Jesus can change the life of someone far from Him or change the heart of someone very near to Him. Do you want to see God change you? This book can help. Not because it has any power in itself, but because it is a vehicle to get you face-to-face with God through His Word.

Are you ready to have your eyes open to what God is doing in and through you? There's no time like now to allow God to reveal Himself to you.

SO, LET'S GET STARTED. LOOK AT THE NEXT PAGE TO LEARN HOW THIS BOOK WORKS.

HOW THIS BOOK WORKS

Here are a few things you need to know to put this book to good use.

START WITH THIS ADVICE
Whether you're super-committed and read your Bible each day or struggle to read a few verses a couple of times a week, the key to sticking with this through four weeks is commitment. Your routine may change, but your commitment to meet God each day has to be there. Tell yourself that whether or not you read this journal at the same time each day, or if you read it whenever you get a few extra minutes, you'll make it a priority in your daily life.

HAVE YOUR BIBLE OPEN
Resist the urge to ignore the spots where this book will tell you to read a passage of Scripture. The close relationship with God that you want only happens by reading and doing what's in the Bible. Have it open as you go through this book.

EACH WEEK IS STRUCTURED THE SAME, BUT IS REALLY DIFFERENT
Each week's content works in similar ways. But, each day is different. And, there are a lot of different kinds of activities. Some will take 3-5 minutes, some 10-15. Some will ask you to look at two or three passages of Scripture; some will just ask you to think about a concept. The variety will make it easier to stick with and help you learn in different ways that are suited to you.

WHAT IF I MISS A DAY OF READING? OR THREE?
Don't give up! Take this at your pace! The goal is for you to grow closer to God. If you miss a day or two . . . or four . . . don't throw in the towel. Pick this book back up and start where you left off. You can do this! And by doing it, you'll show the world that God makes an incredible difference in the lives of His followers. So, hang in there! You've got this!

WELL, THAT'S WHAT YOU NEED TO KNOW TO GET STARTED! TURN THE PAGE TO READ THE INTRODUCTION TO WEEK 1.

WEEK ONE

intro

What's your dad like?

Now that's a loaded question, isn't it?

For some of you, reading this question made you light up. Your dad, while not perfect, is awesome. It's easy to think about how funny or goofy or smart he is. For some of you, this was a painful question. Your dad may be someone who is responsible for causing you a lot of pain. For you, thinking about your dad is really, really hard. And for others of you, thinking about your dad doesn't make you feel anything. You don't know your dad. He's not a factor in your life.

Regardless of how you feel about your dad, there is a truth that should make any of us feel all warm and tingly inside. The truth is that if you have come to faith in Jesus, you have been adopted by a Father who loves you so much you can't possibly even fathom it. He is a perfect, loving, gracious dad who knows you and values you immensely. This week you'll be focusing some on God as your Heavenly Father. Hopefully, it will be a time where you see God in a way that maybe you haven't seen Him before.

I Can Only Imagine deals so much with the feelings we have for our dads. In Bart's story, his feelings changed for his dad as God changed the life of Bart's father. In the place of painful feelings toward his dad, Bart felt love. Only God can bring about this type of change. This week as you learn about God as your Heavenly Father, don't miss what He may be trying to show you about how you feel about your earthly father. Let God work in your life. You may be surprised what He's capable of doing in your life.

IF YOU'RE READY TO GET STARTED, TURN TO PAGE 12 FOR WEEK 1, DAY 1.

WEEK ONE
day one

Read today's devotion and answer the questions to help you think about what it means to love God and love others.

Imagine this; someone approaches you and tells you they want to give you 10 million dollars, but they tell you the money comes with a catch. If you can give away the 10 million by the end of the day, you'll receive another 10 million to keep. The other catch is that you can only give 1,000 dollars away to each person you encounter.

Are you envisioning the smile on people's faces when you hand them 1,000 dollars for absolutely no reason?

Now, what does this scenario have to do with us in reality? We know from the Bible that we have a gift to give that can bring even more happiness than 1,000 dollars: God's love. In the book of 1 John, the author is trying to affirm Christians in their walk with Christ by having them look back at their own lives. Take a moment and read 1 John 4:15-20. Here it states that we have come to know that God loves us. God loves us! But more than this, because God loves us we must love others. If we have loved anyone, then we have known God's love for us.

What do you think it means to love others? Recall a time when you showed love and kindness to someone else. Write about it below if you want.

When we love others, we are experiencing just a small sample of the love that Christ has shown us. Sometimes though, we best understand love when we see a lack of it. Take a moment to write about a time that you felt unloved by someone.

God's love is the greatest thing that we can ever receive. We know that God will always love us, so when we feel alone in this world, we can never forget that Christ died for us because He loves us. Not only is Christ's love the greatest thing we can receive, but it is also the greatest thing we can give. Remember the joy in the faces of those imaginary people we were giving money to in the beginning? Money will fade, but the love of Christ is eternal! Christ comes to us and tells us that we are to show His love to everyone we encounter, so what are you waiting for?

READ THE FOLLOWING QUESTIONS AND LET THEM GUIDE YOU AS YOU THINK ABOUT APPLYING THE TRUTHS OF TODAY'S DEVOTIONAL TO YOUR LIFE.

1. What are some ways that you can show love to a friend today?

2. Is there someone in your life that does not appear to receive a lot of love or kindness from others? Maybe this person is difficult to love. (Maybe this person even reminds you of Bart's dad in the movie.) What can you do to help that person today?

3. What are some ways that you have seen God love you in your own life recently?

4. What are some ways that you can show God's love today in how you act?

WEEK ONE

Read the devotion below and answer the questions on page 15.

Do you remember in elementary school when you would bring store-bought Valentine's Day cards to school with you? Whether they were superheroes, princesses, animals, or even Disney they were all filled with puns about the characters and Valentine's Day. The candy attached to the card was great, but the best feeling was knowing this truth for a moment: someone cared about you.

Have you ever asked yourself that question before? "Does anyone care about me?" Take a moment to read 1 John 4:7-10 for the answer to this question.

After reading this, do you think someone cares about you? Yes or Yes (Circle the answer.)

You might be asking, why did I have to circle it if the answers are both yes? Sometimes when life gets hard, we forget that someone is always looking out for us. That person is Jesus. We want you to have this reminder circled in front of you to answer that question whenever it arises in your life. Does someone care about you? YES!

What you read today in 1 John is that God loves you. He loves you so much that He sent His Son, Jesus, to be a sacrifice in your place so that, if you come to saving faith in Him, your sin doesn't have to separate you from God eternally. That is love!

Our lives are full of expressions of God's love. When things are going great, it can feel like Valentine's Day every day. But what about the hard times? It is OK to think about those too. There are times in our lives where it doesn't seem that anyone is looking out for us or cares about us. There may even be times when those we are supposed to be able to turn to for love and support aren't there for us. But no matter how bad things get, we know God loves us. He loves us unfailingly. No matter what life throws at us, we can count on God's love to sustain us.

Go back and look at 1 John 4:7-10 one more time. Then, answer the questions below:

1. Look at verse 7. How do we know that God is working in and through our lives?

2. Why is it so hard to love others who don't show us love in return? Why is it particularly hard to love those types of people who are particularly close to us (i.e., family members, etc.)?

3. Are there times in your life where you don't feel valued by people you love? What in these verses should help you feel valued no matter what?

4. Spend some time in prayer today thanking God for the people in your life who love you, and asking Him to show you people who need to feel loved by you.

WEEK ONE

Day Three

Read today's devotion and answer the questions on page 17.

Take a moment and imagine that you are making dinner for yourself in your kitchen. Everything is normal until you hear the doorbell ring, and standing at the door is TV chef, Bobby Flay. Bobby says that he heard about your cooking, and he wants to come and eat a meal straight from your incredible kitchen. Do you feel overwhelmed yet? How did Bobby Flay even hear about you? It might feel pretty confusing to have a legend walk into your life to ask you for help. There is a similar scene in the book of Matthew between Jesus and John the Baptist.

Take a moment and read Matthew 3:13-17.

In this passage, John immediately questions Jesus, stating his inadequacies to baptize Jesus. Jesus stops him and says that it is fitting for John to perform this baptism. After Jesus is baptized this incredible moment happens where the skies open up, and the Spirit of God comes down. This had to have been shocking to everyone who witnessed it. We have spent some time this week looking back in our lives to remember moments of love from the Lord, but today we want to start taking steps toward the future.

John tried to stop the moment that was about to come by saying how inadequate he was compared to Jesus. John's shortcomings were not important; it was his faithfulness to do what Jesus was asking him to do that mattered. So often Jesus has excellent things He wants to do in and through us, but we are stuck looking at ourselves rather than Jesus calling us to move. John's ministry for the rest of his life was confirmed and enhanced because he was the one to baptize Jesus, and this one act of faithfulness opened countless doors for the Kingdom of God in the future.

So how about you? What has Jesus called you to do lately? Perhaps you don't feel called to act because you've forgotten what a Holy God Jesus is. Or maybe you don't think God can use you.

1. Look back at verse 17. Write down what God the Father said about Jesus, the Son.

2. What did it mean that God was saying that about Jesus?

3. If you have come to saving faith in Jesus, did you know that God the Father sees you as a beloved child in whom He is well pleased, not because of anything you've done, but because of what Jesus did for you on the cross? It's true. God is so well pleased with you. What does it mean to you that God the Father looks at you as a precious child in whom He delights?

4. How does this approval change the way you see yourself as someone who can be used by God?

5. What does it make you feel like to know God is in your corner?

6. Wrap up today's time of devotion by praying to God, your Heavenly Father, and thanking Him for His love for you.

WEEK ONE / day four

Read the devotion below and answer the questions on page 19.

Is it hard for you to think of God as a loving father? Maybe it's because the concept is too abstract. Or maybe it's because we see too many examples all around us of parents who aren't that loving. Regardless of what we think, the truth is that God is, in fact, a loving Father. The Bible helps us see this over and over again.

One of the most powerful ways in which we see this is in the Parable of the Prodigal Son. While this may be a familiar passage to you, take the time to read Luke 15:11-32. Jesus often taught in stories or parables to give the people listening something familiar and easy to digest, but yet still full of truth. Read the story and think about what Jesus is trying to teach us.

Too often we focus on the wrong aspect of this story. The story highlights a man with two sons, and one of the sons decides to leave home and claim his inheritance early. Often readers focus on the despair this son soon finds himself in, and his willingness to return home. The father welcomes him with open arms, and the son's wrong actions are forgotten when the focus then shifts to the other brother. The other brother is jealous of the attention his younger brother gets upon returning home.

Use the space below to write about which brother you relate best to and why. The brother who regrets his mistakes, or the brother who wants all the love for himself rather than others?

We often focus on the brothers while we forget about the real hero of the story: the father. It's easy for us to look past the actions of the father, but the actions of the father are the truth that Jesus was trying to convey! The father welcomed his lost son when he returned. He forgave his other son for his jealous heart, and he loved both regardless of their actions.

It's difficult to sometimes think about God as the father in the story because we don't think about our sinfulness in the way God does. We can't quite wrap our heads around just how bad our sin is. And when we come to faith in Christ, God the Father just wipes the guilt of that sin away. It's easy for us to forget what an unbelievable, life-changing, earth-shaking truth this is.

1. God is your loving father. You are His child. Take some time to think about all the good blessings God has filled your life with. Write them in the space below:

2. How has God been like the father in the parable in your life?

3. What does it mean to you that God is, in fact, your perfect, loving, Heavenly Father?

Thank God today that He seeks you out, just like the father in the parable, surrounding you with His love no matter what you may have done to let Him down.

WEEK ONE day five

Read today's devotion and answer the questions on page 21.

How confident are you that you breathe the best way possible? Breathing is a vital function of life, and yet it is something that no one ever "teaches" us how to do. The only time we focus on our breathing is when abnormalities occur. There is no point in which you take a class on how to breathe. It's just assumed that you know how to do it.

Let's ask the question again, how confident are you that you breathe the best way possible? If there was a better way to breathe, would you want to know?

Often in our spiritual lives, we can treat prayer like breathing. People spend time learning how to share their faith or defend their faith, but how many people spend time focusing on prayer?

During one of His most well-known sermons, the Sermon on the Mount, Jesus gives a guideline for the proper way to pray. Go ahead and read Matthew 6:6-13. What are some of the things Jesus talks about as being important before we even think about the words to pray? Jot some of those principles below:

Jesus does something extraordinary when He gives us the opening line of the model prayer; He describes God as our Father in heaven. We don't have to ask special permission to go before the Lord, the creator of the world when we want to pray. We merely have to speak, and the being that holds the very fabric of this world together is waiting and listening to us! How cool is that?

Jesus also discusses items such as asking for our daily bread, forgiveness from our sins, and safety from temptation. These are all critical parts of prayer that we should incorporate daily according to Scripture. Was Jesus saying that our prayers that do not follow this model are bad? No way! He was just giving us a model that teaches us how to approach God with our concerns.

Let's ask the question one more time: how good are you at breathing?

Our breath is given to us praise the Lord, and what better way to praise God than by speaking to Him by following His model prayer?

Think about what you just read and answer the questions below:

1. Have you ever thought that you get to approach God in conversation? This should rock our world a bit, shouldn't it? How does Jesus say that we are to address God?

2. What does this say about the role God wants to play in your life?

3. What does a typical prayer look like between you and God? How is it similar/different than the prayer in Matthew?

4. Think back to times when you have seen God answer a prayer of yours. How did that make you feel knowing God was listening?

5. What changes will you make to your own prayer life to follow the example that Jesus gives us in His model prayer?

WEEK ONE day six

Read today's devotion below and write out a prayer to God.

Here we are at the end of our first week of devotions. We've talked about how we know God through love, God's willingness to love and forgive like the father of the prodigal son, and even how we can best communicate with God. More than anything, we've looked at God's role as your Heavenly Father. *I Can Only Imagine* was about the relationship between Bart and his father. As you've thought this week about your relationship with your Heavenly Father, hopefully, you've come to understand God in new and meaningful ways.

Here's a truth that should humble us as believers when we understand how loved we are by God: before the foundations of the world were made God knew He wanted to spend forever with you. If you don't believe that, look at Ephesians 1:4-6. God had a plan for your life before you were even a thought to humanity, and that plan involved being with Him. So, what does that mean for you?

Look again at verse 6. We have one purpose in our lives, and that is to praise the one who adopted us when we didn't deserve it. When we lose sight of this purpose, we fall quickly into the trap of sin and focus on ourselves. We can believe our future is designed to make us great lawyers, politicians, athletes, or business professionals. This was never the purpose of our future; our future was designed to be with the God, the one who chose us over everything else.

As you head into a day of rest and reflection, think about your future. Will your future bring glory to God, or will it feature you as the main star? Take a moment to write out a prayer below asking God to take your future for His glory and to shape it into what best serves His good and perfect will for your life.

WEEK ONE
day seven

TODAY IS A DAY FOR YOU TO REST FROM READING YOUR DAILY DEVOTIONS, BUT NOT FROM MEETING WITH GOD.

If you want, reflect on some of what you have learned. Look back and identify one day in the week that stood out to you. What was it that was so meaningful?

As you go throughout your day, think about what it means that you have God as a good, perfect, and loving Father. How does that change the way you see God and the world around you? Reflect on this truth today.

WEEK TWO *intro*

Why is forgiveness so difficult?

Because it is, right?

One of the hardest things we do as people is looking at someone who has wronged us, really and truly wronged us, and saying, "It's OK. I don't hold it against you." Super, super difficult. It doesn't matter how seemingly insignificant the "wrong" is; forgiving people who have hurt us takes a lot of effort.

Why is forgiveness so hard? Because we mistakenly think that holding someone's mistakes against them gives us power. We believe it puts us in the position of authority like we can decide when they've paid the price of their mistake. The ironic thing is that this only gives that person who wronged us power. It gives their wrong actions power.

Forgiving someone doesn't just free others; it frees you. But it's only something you can do through the power of the Holy Spirit.

Forgiveness is a major theme in *I Can Only Imagine*. It's a current that runs through the movie. It will be your focus this week.

WEEK TWO — day one

Read the devotional below and answer the questions on page 27

Have you ever thought about what it would be like to be famous? Maybe you've imagined yourself as the next sports superstar, artist, or being the best at whatever your craft is. Fame appeals to us, but we rarely think about the effects that fame would have on us if we achieved it. Think about walking down a street and being bombarded by people—not just today, but every day of your life!

In Mark 2:1-12, we find Jesus in this exact same position. Take some time to go ahead and read the passage. The word about Jesus had spread. The chatter of Jesus' miracles was all the rage of the town. Verses 1-2 tell us Jesus is back in Capernaum, and that people are packed wall-to-wall to hear Him preach.

Verses 3-4 describe an account of a band of friends that take it upon themselves to bring their paralyzed friend to Jesus. They knew that Jesus was his only hope of physical healing. After being blocked by the crowd, they climb on top of the roof, remove it, and lower him down. Wow, now that is a group of loyal friends!

What happens next can be confusing, but it is vitally important to understand. Before Jesus heals the man of his paralysis, He tells the disabled man that his sins are forgiven. Why would Jesus do this? Well, Jesus was making a claim about His divinity and the condition of people's hearts. He was confronting the unbelieving skeptics in the crowd by affirming that He was, in fact, God. He was also demonstrating that man's most significant need is forgiveness from an Almighty God.

Take some time to remember your own salvation story. Do you remember the deep sense of guilt that your sin caused, but the overwhelming feeling of God's grace and love? As Christ-followers, we are called to reflect on the depth of forgiveness that God has shown us and go and do likewise. Matthew 18:22 teaches us that withholding forgiveness from our neighbor is not an option. Our lives are called to match the depth of forgiveness found in Christ which is incalculable.

Forgiveness is one of the major themes of *I Can Only Imagine*. Not only did we watch as God forgave Bart's dad, but we also watched as God worked forgiveness in Bart's heart. As you consider the concept of forgiveness, take some time to dive into these questions.

1. Why is seeking God's forgiveness of our sins first and foremost before we can extend forgiveness to our neighbor?

2. Write down a time in which you were forgiven and could not fix the situation. How did it feel to be forgiven?

3. In your own words, write down what happens when a person chooses to forgive another instead of holding their trespass against them.

4. When you pray today, don't spend a lot of time talking to God. Simply thank Him for the forgiveness only He can offer. Then sit quietly and listen to God. Even if God is silent, rest knowing that the forgiveness He provides you means that you have peace with Him.

WEEK TWO

Read the following devotional and answer the questions. Consider writing your answers down in the space provided.

In the movie, *How The Grinch Stole Christmas*, the Grinch has an unfortunate childhood. He looks different from the other children and they mock him for it. However, he thinks his favor is about to turn when his crush, Martha, shows interest in him. He crafts a homemade Christmas gift for her, and the night before he gives it to her, he shaves his face. The next day that he shows up to school, his classmates mercilessly mock and bully him due to his hack job with the razor. From that moment forward, the Grinch allows anger and bitterness to set in. Unforgiveness dominates his heart and leads to isolation from the rest of the community.

Read Matthew 6:14-15. In this passage, Jesus makes it clear that if we do not forgive those who have sinned against us, then our sins are not forgiven. On the contrary, the Lord graciously forgives our sins when we forgive others. It's pretty straightforward.

While we live on this side of eternity, we are bound to experience pain and disappointment at the hands of others. People are imperfect and will wrong us, eventually. (And while we don't like to think about it, we mistreat others as well.) The question that we face is, "What will we do with this hurt?"

In the space below, search your heart and see if there is anything that you have not forgiven someone for. Write those down.

A quote by an unknown author says, "Not forgiving someone is like drinking poison and expecting the other person to die." What does the author mean here?

You know the story: after a devious plan to steal Christmas, the Grinch is confronted by the steadfast love of a little girl named Cindy Lou Who. She perseveres in showing the Grinch kindness and in the end, his heart grows, and he is brought back into community with the town. How does this story parallel the Gospel and what can we learn from it?

Is there someone in your world who needs your forgiveness? What will it take for you to give it to them?

WEEK TWO day Three

Read today's devotion and spend some time with God in prayer.

Take some time to read this quote by Andy Stanley, a pastor from Atlanta:

> "IN THE SHADOW OF MY HURT, FORGIVENESS FEELS LIKE A DECISION TO REWARD MY ENEMY. BUT IN THE SHADOW OF THE CROSS, FORGIVENESS IS MERELY A GIFT FROM ONE UNDESERVING SOUL TO ANOTHER."

I want to challenge you to memorize this quote before you read the rest of the devotional. Let its truth permeate your soul.

Now, we need to address the fact that forgiveness is not easy. In fact, it is impossible without the Holy Spirit enabling you to forgive. In our flesh, we operate under Hammurabi's code which says, "an eye for an eye and a tooth for a tooth." However, Jesus says in Matthew 5:39, "But if anyone slaps you on the right cheek, turn to him the other also." In this situation, our natural reaction would be to fight or take flight, but Jesus commands neither of those actions. He calls us to stand firm, love our enemies, and to become ambassadors of forgiveness.

Go ahead and read Luke 7:36-50. Here, we find an immoral woman who hears that Jesus is dining in a Pharisee's house. The pain of her decisions has left her life in shambles. But in Christ, she sees the offer of hope and redemption from the pain of her past. Instead of despising those who have hurt her, she looks to the Savior to find healing from her sins and the aftermath of those who have sinned against her.

The parable following the account of the woman with the alabaster jar teaches us that we can undervalue forgiveness. Satan would love for us to fall into the trap of treating forgiveness casually, eventually causing our hearts to become calloused. The way to overcome the enemy's tactics is to remember who we were before Christ—broken, enslaved to sin, and with no hope. Then, we reflect on the grace and mercy that God had for us by rescuing us through Christ!

As a result of this grand salvation, we become imitators of Christ. We forgive each other because we did not deserve to be forgiven by God. Although we still experience the sting of others' offenses towards us, anger or bitterness doesn't control us. Instead, we are compelled to forgive by love.

Think about what Bart's father had put him through. Think of all the hurt and pain. How could Bart ultimately forgive his dad? Only because of the power of God in Him. Bart couldn't forgive unless he was forgiven first and given the freedom by God to forgive others.

As we wrap up the devotional for today, write a short prayer that encapsulates your need of forgiveness from the Lord and your commission to forgive others. Use the space below.

WEEK TWO of four

Read the devotional below and consider the scenario on page 33.

Go ahead and dive into 2 Corinthians 5:19-20 and Matthew 18:21-22 for our reading today.

Do you know what an ambassador does? They speak and act on behalf of another person, group, or organization. To put this in perspective, an ambassador of the U.S. has the power to make vital decisions and to form policy with other nations that directly impacts the well-being of the United States.

You may think this a distant concept, but I'm willing to bet you have ambassadors all around. The captains of the football team, the class president, the leaders of school clubs—they all represent their different groups and act in their best interest.

Likewise, our passages show us that God has purposed us to serve the role of ambassador. Christ-followers are always in the business of reconciliation. Whether it is introducing someone to Jesus or solving a dispute between one another, we are always pointing back to the Gospel for all things.

For the remainder of today's devotion, you will read a fictional scenario and respond in your own words.

"Tyson, Katherine, and Josie have all been close since their 8th-grade year. They originally all met at their Wednesday night youth group service and have stayed committed to each other as friends ever since. For the past four years, they've been inseparable. Early on, as they began to grow in their friendship, they frequently had deep spiritual conversations and invited each other into accountability. However, now that junior year has arrived, Tyson and Katherine have started to see a change in Josie. Josie has started hanging out with the party crowd. She's stopped responding to Tyson and Katherine's texts and avoids them at school. Finally, they were able to track her down after school one day. Josie totally went off on them. Josie told them that they never really were her friends in the first place. She tells them to stop texting her. Both Tyson and Katherine are shocked and hurt."

In the space below, I want you to put yourself in Tyson and Katherine's shoes. Respond to the questions below.

1. How does Matthew 18:21-22 inform how we treat this situation?

2. What are some things that you could do to remind Josie that she is loved?

3. If Josie decided to meet for coffee and hear you out, what would you say to her that would reflect being an 'ambassador of reconciliation'?

WEEK TWO day five

Read the devotion below and answer the questions on page 35.

In Taylor Swift's hit song, "Look What You Made Me Do," she sings about a person that has left a deep emotional scar on her life. Instead of opting to forgive her betrayer, she chooses to rely on "karma" and her own ability to move beyond the pain.

While we can relate to Swift's response (we're human after all), it's not the response that we have observed this week in our devotionals. It's not the kind of response that Scripture advocates. Christians are implored to let quarrels and contentions die and to seek unity with one another. However, if we are to succeed in this lifestyle, our ability to forgive must be rooted somewhere other than our own willpower.

Take a moment and read Luke 23:6-49. It's a longer passage so take your time. In verses 6-16, Jesus is put on trial before Pilate and Herod. They interrogated Jesus, yet He was deemed to be innocent by both of these rulers. However, the Jewish religious leaders were insistent on putting Jesus to death. To seize the moment, they all cried aloud, "Away with this man, and release to us Barabbas." During the Passover, it was a custom that a prisoner should be released. To keep the peace, Pilate caved and exchanged the guilty Barabbas for Jesus who stood innocent.

Verses 26-49 portray the gruesome death of Christ. He is beaten, mocked, and nailed to a cross. In the midst of humanity's darkest day, Jesus does not succumb to the evil He experiences. It was quite the opposite when He prays for those crucifying Him, "Father, forgive them, for they do not know what they do."

Even more than that, we find Jesus forgiving one of the repentant robbers who was being crucified alongside him in verse 43.

So where do we find our basis of forgiveness? It's found in the cross.

It's found in the Son of God who subjected Himself to death for our sake.

Take heart; if you believe in Jesus then your sins are no longer held against you!

It is only when we understand the depth of Christ's forgiveness for us that we can begin to forgive others. You may be surprised to find out that true forgiveness not only changes you, but it changes your accusers too.

Take some time to engage with these questions:

1. Why must our forgiveness be rooted in the cross?

2. What is the hardest part of forgiveness for you?

3. How does prayer play a part in forgiving others?

4. Why is it dangerous to hold onto grudges?

WEEK TWO *day six*

How do we react to those people who seem hard to love? Like God does.

In *The Lion, The Witch, And The Wardrobe*, Edmund appears to be so corrupted that he cannot be rescued. The White Witch has cast her spell upon him, and he has sold out to the dark side. He's left his sisters and brother in pursuit of his pleasure. By all standards, Edmund has created his demise, and he deserves it.

However, Aslan, the symbolic God-figure in Narnia, does not give up on Edmund so easily. He goes as far as to substitute his own life in place of Edmund's. In this process, Edmund is shown true love and is won back. His life is redeemed and given purpose.

Read Luke 15:3-7. How often do we give up on people who appear to be too far from God? The Kingdom of God proclaims that no one is a lost cause. In our passage today, the shepherd sets aside 99 sheep to go in search of the one. When the lost sheep is found, the shepherd calls for a party to rejoice its return back to the flock!

God's heart for the lost cannot be overstated. He pursues those who have no regard for Him because He loves them. Verse 7 shows us that when the one who was lost is found, heaven erupts in joy.

Now imagine if our lives resembled God's heart for those that are far from Him. What if we used the rejection of others as motivation to continue to embody God's love in their life? The truth is that no one is too far from God. The worst person that you know is still capable of coming to salvation and living a transformed life.

The question is, "Will you live a life overflowing with grace and mercy that draws people to the hope that you have?" It's not easy, but it's definitely worth the struggle. Remember that the battle is not won by how hard you fight, but rather who fights for you.

The activity for today is to think about those you would classify as far from God, the 'Edmunds' of your life, and pray that God would do a miraculous work in their heart.

WEEK TWO of seven

TAKE TODAY OFF . . . REALLY. TAKE A BREAK.

But don't stop thinking about God today. Don't stop listening to Him. Especially as He reminds you of how He has changed your life through the power of the Gospel.

Take some time today and soak in the world around you. See God in His creation. Thank Him for it. And praise Him by having as much fun today as you possibly can.

WEEK THREE *intro*

What does the word "redemption" mean?

Redemption is the act of having freedom purchased or wholeness restored through a significant payment. OK. Got it. But what does that mean when applied to our lives?

We can't discuss redemption without starting with a foundation of brokenness. We are broken. We are sinful. Apart from God, our sin devalues us. But through faith in Jesus' sacrificial work on the cross, God made it possible for our life to have value.

God purchased us from sin and death through the blood shed by Jesus on the cross. He bought us. For all who believe in Him, God gives us the right to become His children. We are His. Our lives have been redeemed.

I Can Only Imagine is a powerful story of redemption. God redeemed Bart from his sins as a child when Bart came to faith in Him. Bart's dad was redeemed from his sins when he came to faith in Christ as an adult. And because God is a God of redemption, He redeemed Bart and his father's relationship through grace, love, and forgiveness.

This week is all about the concept of redemption and how we see it in Scripture. Enjoy this week as you consider the new value and meaning God has purchased for you through Christ.

WEEK THREE / day one

Read today's devotional thought and spend time reflecting on the questions on page 41.

Does it seem to you like every single month there is a new superhero movie premiering in theatres? Now, everyone loves a good superhero movie. But when we look a little closer, it seems like every superhero movie has the same basic storyline. Think about it: an ordinary man or woman leads a normal life, some catastrophic or life-changing event reorients that individual giving them superhuman abilities, and somewhere along the line they realize that they can use these skills to save and protect the earth from harm.

Seems pretty predictable, doesn't it?

Why then do we continually line up to see these kinds of movies over and over again? The answer is found in a single word: redemption. There is something enticing about a story where someone puts their lives on the line to rescue those who cannot protect themselves. We are attracted to redemptive storylines like these because we are hardwired to long for redemption.

Read Romans 3:23. What does it tell us? It says that we have all sinned and fallen short of God's glory and are all in need of redemption. No one wrote more about this than the apostle Paul in his letters to the churches. We see that Paul teaches that once God decided to redeem and save His people from their sins, He sent His Only Son Jesus Christ as a sacrifice so that by His blood we could be redeemed. Paul makes this clear in Ephesians 1:7. Read that if you want, too. Because of this sacrifice, our salvation and redemption are sealed forever in Him. In Ephesians 1:14 Paul writes that the Holy Spirit is He "who is the guarantee of our inheritance until we acquire possession of it, to the praise of His glory." This means that when we believe in Christ, our inheritance or redemption is forever sealed and assured from the punishment of sin.

Paul teaches that not only does the Holy Spirit empower us to believe and seals our redemption, but He is continually working to redeem and save us each day. Ephesians 4:30 says, "And do not grieve the Holy Spirit of God, by whom you were sealed for the day of redemption." And the best news? Once we are redeemed we are invited to join the family of God and are never enslaved to our sins again (Gal. 4:5; Heb. 9:12).

See? Paul really did write a lot about this! Maybe it's because Paul, like us, knew that he needed the redemption only God can bring about. The fact is, Jesus is the superhero to trump all superheroes. He is the sacrificial Son of God who has saved us from our sins and redeemed us into His family.

1. Take a moment and think back to some of the sins that you have struggled with in recent months. How does it feel to know that God still desires to redeem you in light of these things?

2. Why do you think it is so important that our redemption is sealed in the Holy Spirit forever?

3. Knowing that Jesus redeems us from our sins, how should we live differently in light of our redemption? Write some ideas below.

4. Read Galatians 4:4-5. Why do you think it is significant that we are adopted into God's family? How are you different as a result?

Now, thank God for redeeming and rescuing you from your sins and calling you to faith in Him.

WEEK THREE

Read today's devotional and follow the prompts on page 43.

Everyone loves a good story, but not all stories are created equal. Some are more positive and upbeat; others are more sad and disappointing. Some are full of excitement or comedy, and others are full of drama and heartache. No matter the kinds of stories we like to watch, read or tell, all of us use stories every day.

Some of our favorite stories are those that surprise us, stories that are unpredictable and keep us on the edge of our seats like a suspenseful movie unfolding piece by piece. These are the kinds of stories that we live for. Yesterday we learned that our redemption is accomplished through the greatest true story ever told: the life, death, and resurrection of Jesus. We learned that we are rescued and sealed by Him and redeemed through His blood. But this isn't the only story we have about Jesus. In fact, the Gospels are full of stories of redemption where Jesus redeemed those who were lost and hopeless. Stories full of suspense and excitement!

We see one of these stories in Matthew 8:1-4. Take a moment and read this story in your Bible. Here we learn that because of His teaching and miracles, many people were following Jesus. Among these people, the Scriptures tell us there was a leper who came before Jesus. Leprosy was a skin disease prevalent in Jesus' day that would cause the flesh to rot and become deformed. It was highly contagious and was considered by the Jews to be a sign of God's judgment, resulting in banishment from the community.

Knowing these things, we can see that this man was desperate and hopeless when he falls before Jesus among the crowd.

When the leper asks Jesus to heal him, Jesus stretches out His hand, and the man is made clean! What a story of redemption! The Gospels are full of stories like this where hopeless people are redeemed and cleansed by Jesus. There are numerous stories of redemption full of suspense, drama, and surprise, and they bring great joy and peace to those of us who have also been redeemed by Jesus.

Where did you see redemption in *I Can Only Imagine?* There were quite a few examples. Primarily, we see both Bart and his father redeemed by Christ when they came to saving faith in Jesus. We see God redeem their relationship, as well. But there is more. God redeemed Bart's story, giving Bart a powerful song that connected with millions and millions of people.

Redemption is a powerful theme God works in the lives of His children. In the space below, take a moment and write out your story of redemption. Include where you were, who was there, and what took place. Write down how you felt when you surrendered to Christ and how you felt when He redeemed you. Once you write, underline the sentence that describes the moment you surrendered your life to Jesus. Then, pray and thank God that like the stories of redemption in Scripture, you too are a part of His great story of redemption that spans across all of human history and beyond.

WEEK THREE

Read today's devotion and think about the questions on page 45.

Take a moment and think of three or four of your favorite memories growing up with your family. Got them? Chances are, at least one of them concerns food in some way, shape, or form. Whether its decorating Christmas cookies in December or a special birthday dinner your family makes you every year, the fact is that there is something special about sharing and connecting over a meal with people we care about.

Yesterday we recalled the meaning of redemption through a better understanding of the stories recorded in the Gospels. When we look at the Gospels at these stories, it's evident that just like today, Jesus utilized meals as a place to connect with people also.

Take a moment and read Mark 2:13-17. What truth can we learn from this story? Jesus didn't come to redeem people who felt that they had it all together. In fact, Jesus came to eat with tax collectors and sinners like Levi; people who wanted to be redeemed and loved, who had lost their way and are enslaved to sin. People just like you.

Before Jesus, you were just like one of these people seated at the table, but Jesus cares for you so much that He redeemed you and welcomed you into His family.

Today's activity is simple: as much as you can, think about what it means to be redeemed from a life of slavery to sin.

Ask yourself the following questions throughout the day. Feel free to write your answers in the space provided.

1. How does it make you feel that Jesus redeemed you in spite of your sin?

2. How should you view others in light of your own redemption?

3. What has changed in your life since you came to faith in Jesus?

4. How can you thank God each day for the redemption you have in Jesus?

In a journal or note-taking app, write down any thoughts these questions stir in you.

WEEK THREE of four

Read the devotional below and answer the questions on page 47.

Let's face it: there is a big difference between knowing something and doing it. For instance, there is a big difference between knowing that you need to eat healthily and refusing to eat a delicious piece of pizza. Or how about the difference between knowing that you should go to bed on time, and putting down the Xbox controller? The fact is many of us know a lot of things! But that doesn't mean we practice those things.

And then, there is rest. Rest is one of the things we know we need but often fail to do. And this isn't just referring to physical rest, but spiritual rest.

Have you ever stopped and thought about how redemption and rest go together? The last few days we have recalled the meaning of redemption and its effect on our lives. Redemption was never meant to be a one-time, over and done experience but something that affects us here and now, every day. In the busyness of life, our tendency is to try to earn our way, to show our ability, to work fast and hard. But the Bible teaches us something different. We need rest.

Take a moment and read Matthew 12:1-8. Jesus and His disciples were hungry. As they were walking among the fields on the Sabbath day, He and His disciples began to pluck heads of grain for them to eat, but the Pharisees were watching. The Pharisees accused Jesus and His disciples of breaking God's law that the people were not to work on the Sabbath. The truth is, the Pharisees were all about performance.

Jesus sees right through the Pharisees' self-righteousness and accuses them of being people who are so concerned about their performance that they missed the whole point of God's law in the first place. God is not concerned about our level of busyness. He is concerned about us.

The good news of the Gospel is that for those who are redeemed, we are no longer measured by whether we perform well or not. Instead, the Gospel reorients us to rest in who God has made us in Christ Jesus. Knowing that we need to rest in the Gospel is one thing, but reorienting our lives so that we are constantly at rest in the Gospel is what God desires most for us.

Take a moment and write down all of the things that take up the most time in your life each day. Now circle all of the words that cannot change your standing with God.

All of your words should be circled! There is nothing that can change your standing with God; so rest in the good news of the Gospel today.

SPEND SOME TIME IN PRAYER TODAY CONSIDERING ALL THAT GOD HAS DONE FOR YOU. PRAISE HIM FOR HIS LOVE FOR YOU THAT ISN'T PERFORMANCE BASED. THANK HIM FOR UNCONDITIONALLY LOVING YOU.

WEEK THREE day five

Read the devotional below and answer the questions on the following page.

Oftentimes GPS feels like more of a pain than a help. Everyone knows what GPS is supposed to do: to get you from point A to point B as quickly as possible. Every once in a while, however, your GPS app seems to take you in a direction that seems totally ridiculous and unneeded. You think to yourself, "Why in the world am I going down this backstreet?" Or maybe you ask, "Why am I driving away from where I need to be going?"

Most people who use GPS probably think they know better than the app in the first place. But the truth is, Google Maps knows more than us. Seriously! It knows where there are slowdowns, construction projects, accidents, and closed roads. It knows when traffic is bad and whether or not it's faster to take the Interstate or streets, but some people still constantly question its directions. What's the point?

We often do the very same thing to God. He may be the one who redeemed and rescued us, who by His own power saved us from our sins. He may be a perfect and all-knowing God who created the universe, but when things don't go our way, what do we do? We question Him as if He were a GPS app giving us questionable directions.

If we are completely honest though, we often don't understand God's ways. In Him, freedom doesn't come from control but obedience. He sees the big picture, whereas we see just what's in front of our faces. Take for example some of the teachings of Jesus. Jesus essentially said, "the first shall be last," and "power comes through weakness." These may make no sense to the world, but God's wisdom is far beyond our own.

A perfect example of this is in Matthew 26:17-25. Read this passage to yourself.

Here we have the story of the Last Supper where Jesus informs His disciples, those closest to Him, that one of them would betray Him. Confused and concerned, the disciples begin to try and discover who it might be. They were completely confused! How could one of them betray Jesus? And why would the Son of God die?

We see in Scripture that the disciples would look back on this moment with Jesus after His death and finally put the pieces together. Jesus knew things that they did not know. He knew what would happen even before He was taken to His death. What does this mean for us? The wisdom of Christ is far above our own, and God's ways are far higher than ours.

Instead of questioning God, let's trust and follow the directions He gives. He knows better than us where we are going.

Think about the following questions. Answer them in the space provided if you choose.

1. Are there areas in your life right now that feel out of your control? What are they?

2. In what ways can you give these areas to God and release your worry and doubt to Him?

3. How does your redemption in Jesus Christ affect the way that you face adversity in your life? Explain.

4. What are some practical things you can do now to be obedient to God in the hard areas of your life?

WEEK THREE *of six*

Read today's devotional and think about how its truth impacts your life.

Think of a time when you were forgiven for something for which you did not deserve forgiveness. Think of the feeling that you felt when that person released you from your mistake and forgave you for the pain that you caused them. What kinds of emotions did you feel? What did you want to do in response?

The truth is that the emotions we felt when forgiven for our mistake are only a taste of the full forgiveness that Jesus offers to us in the Gospel. Because we are covered by the blood of Jesus, the mortal punishment that we deserve for our sins is washed away. We are able not only to be forgiven but to be welcomed into the family of God! What amazing news this is!

Songs and music, in general, are gifts from God which have been given to us to praise Him for the redemption He offers. Songs have a way of connecting with our minds and our hearts. They give language to our feelings and allow us to express our gratitude for the grace that is given freely to us.

In fact, songs are present throughout Scripture. Take a moment and read Psalm 103:1-6.

What a list of blessings from God! When we read of all God has done for us, how can we not sing? The psalms are full of these kinds of songs of praise which recount all that God has done for us through the redemption that we receive in Jesus Christ. No matter where we are in our life, whether we are happy or disappointed, we can still sing. How? Because we have a hope that looks beyond this world. We know that we are redeemed in Jesus, children in God's family, and that one day we will be with God in heaven forever.

Let us not neglect the forgiveness that we have been shown. Instead, let's sing songs of praise and thanks to God who will one day return and make all things new.

Today, keep this thought in the front of your mind: One day, all struggle and pain and disappointment will be wiped away forever, and those who know Jesus will sing His praise and be with Him.

WEEK THREE *day seven*

When God rested on the seventh day during creation, He was prescribing a wonderful exercise that He wanted His people to also adhere to: rest is holy.

Sometimes we think of rest as laziness, and to be sure, just like everything not done in moderation, too much rest can cross over into apathy and sloth. A Sabbath is a reset of our hearts, minds, and bodies. It's crucial to the rhythms of our lives, both as humans and as spiritual beings.

So today, we Sabbath, taking some time to rest and recharge. Use some of this time to think back over what you've learned this week, and how God encountered you.

WEEK FOUR *intro*

Home. The word is supposed to bring about emotions in us that are all warm and cozy. For some people, what you know as "home" doesn't have quite the positive vibe to it. For others, the word home does just that. Home is a healthy, safe, even fun place.

The concept of home is different to different people.

But to those who have been saved by faith in Christ, home is a pretty cool word to consider.

Do you know what the Bible says about your true home? Maybe you do, maybe you don't. You will after reading this week's devotions, and what you'll find is that the Bible has plenty to say about it. For anyone who has come to saving faith in Jesus, God has a home for you, both today in this world and the future in Heaven. But we're getting ahead of ourselves.

Think about your home. Think about how you saw the idea of "home" portrayed in *I Can Only Imagine*. It was a moving target, wasn't it? For most of the parts of Bart's life we saw portrayed in the movie, home was a place of sorrow and pain. But that changed. By the end of the film, home was a place of peace and joy. What happened to cause this change? God happened.

God has the power to make any place a place of refuge. That's what home truly is: a place where you can safely rest.

This week we'll see how God changes the concept of home. Ready? Let's jump in.

WEEK FOUR — day one

Read the devotion below and answer the questions on page 55.

Where is home for you?

How do you even answer that question? Did you think of a city first? Or did you visualize the building in which you live?

Regardless of what you live in, the majority of people reading this book will have a place they call home. It may be a house, an apartment, or a mobile home. Home for you might even be as simple as a couch. Regardless, most of you have a home. And homes are essential, to the point that when people find themselves "homeless," it's a problem. Since people were cavemen, we've been drawn to the idea of a home, a place of safety and refuge.

As mentioned in the introduction, the final week of this book is about the concept of home. As we begin to unpack what this looks like, there's kind of an important point to deal with right out of the gate: While Jesus was on earth, He didn't have a home. He was essentially homeless. Seriously. Don't believe it? He said it Himself:

"And Jesus said to him, "Foxes have holes, and birds of the air have nests, but the Son of Man has nowhere to lay his head." - Matthew 8:20

How is it that the Son of God didn't have a place to call home? Of all the people to ever walk this earth, He's the ONE person who most deserved a home. In fact, when you consider this for a moment, it makes what Jesus did by coming to earth in the first place all the more meaningful. He walked out of Heaven, where He was the object of worship, to step into a world where He didn't even have a home. Amazing. But this all begins to make sense when you think about the two ways Jesus talked about His "home."

The main way Jesus spoke of "home" was to point to a future time when He would rejoin God the Father in Heaven and ultimately bring all His children to dwell forever with Him. We'll get to that later in the week. But the other way Jesus spoke of home was in the hearts of those who followed Him.

Take a moment and read John 14:22–24. Here it is to make it easier for you:

> [22] Judas (not Iscariot) said to him, 'Lord, how is it that you will manifest yourself to us, and not to the world?' [23] Jesus answered him, "If anyone loves me, he will keep my word, and my Father will love him, and we will come to him and make our home with him. [24] Whoever does not love me does not keep my words. And the word that you hear is not mine but the Father's who sent me.

Look at verse 23. What does Jesus say about where His "home" is?

What is the requirement for God making His home within you?

What do you think it means that God would "make [His] home with [you]"?

Jesus made it clear to us. He may not have had a home while He was on earth, but to all those who would believe in Him, Jesus dwells within them. God, in the form of the Holy Spirit, lives within all Believers. It's God's way of assuring us that we're His until we join Him in Heaven. In this way, God has a "home" in you. As God, Jesus could say this with confidence. Jesus' earthly "home" was in the heart of those who loved and followed Him.

If you have come to saving faith in Jesus, God is with you. The Spirit dwells inside of you. You are never far from God. What an amazing promise this is for all of us. Take some time today and consider this truth. Let it sink in as much as possible. Pray to God and tell Him how it makes you feel knowing that He has made a home in your life.

WEEK FOUR

Read the devotional for today and use the prompts to help you think about how to apply it to your life.

Take a moment and read John 12:26. It's a simple verse, but a powerful one.

Now, write the verse in the space provided.

OK, now, look back at what you just wrote. Circle the command Jesus gave to Believers. What do you think Jesus means when He says to "follow" Him?

Next, draw a box around where Jesus says His followers will be. In your own words, what does it mean to be where Jesus is?

Finally, underline the promise Jesus makes to His followers. What do you think Jesus means when He says that God will honor those who serve Jesus?

When we begin to think about what it means to have a home with Christ, it doesn't mean the house we live in, even if our family is a very godly one. When we think of a home with Jesus, it means being WITH Jesus. Wherever He is.

Where do you see Jesus at work around your community? Are you there with Him? Serving alongside Jesus is part of what it means to be a follower of Christ. We can't believe in Jesus and claim to love Him without being willing to be where He is.

Consider these following questions:
1. Define what home means to you.

2. Where is the intersection in your definition of home and Jesus' desire that you follow Him where He goes?

3. If being with Jesus is part of your identity, what keeps you from following Him more closely?

4. Take some time today and pray, asking Jesus to show you where He is at work around you and giving you the strength to join Him.

WEEK FOUR / Day Three

Read today's devotional and the following quote and answer the questions.

Near the end of His time on earth, Jesus gathered with His disciples at what we now call the Last Supper. It was the last Passover feast Jesus would celebrate with His disciples before His arrest, death, and resurrection. Jesus made it a point to do as He had always done: pour into the disciples, teaching and encouraging them until the very end.

Take a moment and read John 14:1–4. Jesus is talking to His disciples while they were still gathered around the table. Read the following verses and look at what Jesus was telling His followers:

> "Let not your hearts be troubled. Believe in God; believe also in me. In my Father's house are many rooms. If it were not so, would I have told you that I go to prepare a place for you? And if I go and prepare a place for you, I will come again and will take you to myself, that where I am you may be also. And you know the way to where I am going." - John 14:1–4

There are two main truths here. See if you can write them down in the space below:

Did you catch them? Jesus focused on two things here: that He was going to prepare a place for them in "[His] Father's house," and that He would be returning to bring them to be with Him. Jesus is, of course, talking about Heaven ("my Father's house") and the future home of all of God's children ("that where I am you may be also."). Knowing everything that was about to happen, Jesus was giving His disciples a powerful reminder of the future that awaited them.

The quote below speaks to precisely what Jesus was saying. Read it and respond to the questions that follow it.

"[JESUS] TOLD US—AND IT IS ONLY BECAUSE WE ARE SO ACCUSTOMED TO IT THAT WE DO NOT WONDER MORE AT THE MAGNIFICENCE OF THE CONCEPTION—THAT WHEN OUR PLACE IN THIS WORLD SHOULD KNOW US NO MORE, THERE WOULD BE ANOTHER PLACE READY FOR US." - HENRY DRUMMOND

1. Drummond is talking about Jesus' promise of eternal life with Him for all who believe. Drummond says something about the way we interact with this message. What does he say about how we receive it?

2. Why do you think it's hard for us to fully understand the "magnificence" of Jesus' promise of Heaven?

3. Hope is a huge part of the Gospel. In the Imagine movie, hope is what allows a guy like Bart to be at peace with his father's death. What does Jesus' promise of an eternal home with Him have to do with hope? Why is it something that makes us hopeful?

4. Take some time today and pray to God asking Him to restore to you the wonder of His promise of a future home. Ask Him to help you grasp even a little bit of what it will be like to spend forever in His presence.

WEEK FOUR

Read today's devotion and answer the questions on page 61.

What is the most amazing, most unbelievable story you've ever heard? Maybe it's a kid climbing Mt. Everest. Or maybe it's a story of miraculous survival when death was the only logical outcome. The incredible and outlandish stories are the ones that stick with us. We love them for their unpredictability and their ability to completely blow away our preconceived notions about how a story should play out.

There is a story like this in the Bible. In fact, it's one of the most awesome stories in Scripture, not only for the outcome but for all that we see happening in it. That story is the raising of Lazarus. Take a couple of minutes and read it. It's found in John 11:1-44 (and it is fantastic).

The intro in verses 1-16 is remarkable. Mary and Martha send a messenger to Jesus to tell Him that their brother and Jesus' friend, Lazarus, is dying. What does Jesus do? He waits. He allows Lazarus to die. Why? We could spend a lot more words than we have room for discussing the "whys." Thankfully, Jesus gives us the reason: "It is for the glory of God, so that the Son of God may be glorified through it" (vs. 4). Jesus knew that ultimately God would be glorified through what was going to happen.

Go back and look at that exchange between Jesus and Martha starting in verse 21. Martha is hurting, and she's frustrated that Jesus didn't come sooner. Even in her grief, she knows Jesus is still Lord. Jesus assures her that Lazarus will live again. Martha shows her faith in Jesus and His plan for the future when she says that she believes Lazarus will rise again when Jesus returns to call all His children to Him. Jesus tells her that this isn't exactly what He is talking about, and reminds her who He is with a powerful exclamation:

> "Jesus said to her, 'I am the resurrection and the life. Whoever believes in me, though he die, yet shall he live, and everyone who lives and believes in me shall never die. Do you believe this?'" - John 11:25-26

Jesus goes on to raise Lazarus from the dead, showing His ultimate power over death and sin, and foreshadowing a day when everyone who has been saved by faith will join together with God, defeating death and living in relationship with God forever.

Read the following questions and consider how this narrative impacts your life:

1. Jesus has power over sin and death. Jesus showed this in the story of Lazarus being raised. Can you think of any other places in the Bible where we see this?

2. Jesus says that if we believe in Him, we shall never die. What does that statement mean to you?

3. Jesus died to save us from an eternity separated from Him. When we come to saving faith in Jesus, we are made right with God. Jesus clears the way for us to be in relationship with God for eternity. Our forever-home is with God. How does that make you feel?

4. Your home is not here. It's with God. Forever. How does this truth impact your life on a daily basis?

WEEK FOUR day five

Read the devotional below and spend some time journaling using the prompts on page 63.

Take a moment and read the following verses:

"[1] For we know that if the tent that is our earthly home is destroyed, we have a building from God, a house not made with hands, eternal in the heavens. [2] For in this tent we groan, longing to put on our heavenly dwelling, [3] if indeed by putting it on we may not be found naked. [4] For while we are still in this tent, we groan, being burdened—not that we would be unclothed, but that we would be further clothed, so that what is mortal may be swallowed up by life. [5] He who has prepared us for this very thing is God, who has given us the Spirit as a guarantee.

[6] So we are always of good courage. We know that while we are at home in the body we are away from the Lord, [7] for we walk by faith, not by sight. [8] Yes, we are of good courage, and we would rather be away from the body and at home with the Lord. [9] So whether we are at home or away, we make it our aim to please him. [10] For we must all appear before the judgment seat of Christ, so that each one may receive what is due for what he has done in the body, whether good or evil." - 2 Corinthians 5:1–10

This is the Apostle Paul writing to the Christ-followers in Corinth. He's talking about the tension of living here in this world but longing to be home in our forever-home with God. Paul uses the metaphor of a tent to talk about our bodies.

What does Paul say about our bodies in verse 1?

Verses 2-5 represent Paul talking about the struggle to be stuck in our physical bodies on the earth while knowing that one day we'll be called to our forever-home with God. If you're honest, are there days when it would be a lot easier to leave this world and join God in Heaven? Life can throw us curveballs. Things can go poorly. We can turn around one day and find that we're not having a great time. In those moments, Heaven can seem a lot more appealing than earth. But Paul challenges us to think differently.

Look at verses 6-10. Paul acknowledges that being home with God would be easier. But he says we have to stay here as long as God has us here. We are to be of good courage while we live our lives on earth, making sure we draw others to God with our Christ-centered lives. It's part of our purpose. It's part of why God called us to Him, to be His representatives on this earth.

The space provided below is for you to journal. God knows that life isn't easy. Jesus experienced it first-hand. And God's long-term plan is to have His children live with Him forever. But for now, you are here. God needs you here to shine your light. Spend some time today talking with God about the tension of living with both of these truths. Share your thoughts with Him. Listen to what He's saying to you. Think about it as you go throughout your day.

WEEK FOUR

Read the following devotional and consider how it impacts your life.

One of the best parts of a big trip is the anticipation. You know you're going to get to do this really cool thing. You know at some time in the future, it's going to be a reality. It's a certainty. Your parents have all the arrangements made. For now, you're just waiting.

What is that anticipation like? Some days it's fresh on your mind. The only thing you can think about is the trip. Other days you almost forget about it. Which is CRAZY! But that's how our minds work. Then something happens, and you remember the upcoming trip, and you're excited all over again.

Read Revelation 21:1-4. Here, John is relaying to us a vision God allowed him to have about the future return of God to call all His children to Himself and dwell forever with them. It's a long, fascinating book. The part you just read comes near the very end of the book. In this passage, John saw what he called a "new heaven and a new earth." This is John's way of describing our forever-home with God. It's not a better version of our current home. It's something entirely different.

If we believe in Jesus, we are assured an eternal dwelling place with Him. Look what John wrote in verse 3-4: "Behold, the dwelling place of God is with man. He will dwell with them, and they will be his people, and God himself will be with them as their God. [4] He will wipe away every tear from their eyes, and death shall be no more, neither shall there be mourning, nor crying, nor pain anymore, for the former things have passed away."

The home that is promised to us? Our forever-home? It will be a place where God is personally and physically with us. There will be no suffering, no pain, and no need. This is the home God has in mind for each of His children. It is an awe-inspiring truth about what is to come.

Spend today thinking about this reality. Talk to God and ask Him to give you new insight into how to process this powerful truth. Listen to what He has to say to you. Praise Him for who He is and for His perfect plan for you.

WEEK FOUR / day seven

YOU HAVE ONE TASK FOR TODAY...

Somewhere in the bottom part of this page, summarize what you've learned over the past four weeks in one sentence.

Think about this concept as you go through the next couple of days. Consider how it has impacted your understanding of faith.

NOTES

NOTES

Acknowledgments

This book was written by the following team of authors:

ANDY BLANKS
Andy is the Co-Founder and Publisher for YM360. Andy lives in Birmingham, AL with his wonderful wife Brendt, their three daughters, and one son. He's a pretty big fan of both the Boston Red Sox and anything involving the Auburn Tigers. When he's not hanging out with his family or volunteering at his church's youth ministry, you can find Andy trail running or mountain biking.

ROBBIE CRAWFORD
Robbie and his wife Lindsay currently serve in youth ministry in Birmingham, AL. He works primarily with middle school students because he believes students of that age will be the ones who change the world. Robbie is a kid at heart, and loves spending time having fun with friends and family.

JEREMY HORTON
Jeremy is a children's minister in Birmingham, AL and loves everything about sharing the Good News of Jesus with kids and teens. He is husband to Anna, father to Abraham, and enjoys riding his road bike or going for a run. If Jeremy could be one thing when he grows up, he would be a National Parks Ranger and just go camping all the time. What could be better than that?

CLAY WYATT
Clay grew up in Albany, GA and has played baseball, basketball, and ping pong for as long as he can remember. During college, he pursued both journalism and theology, and loves the opportunity to merge both of these passions in projects like this journal. Clay serves on the staff of Shades Mountain Baptist Church in Birmingham, AL, and will graduate in 2018 from Beeson Divinity School.

Also contributing to creation of this project:
EXECUTIVE EDITOR: ANDY BLANKS
ART DIRECTOR: LAUREL-DAWN LATSHAW
PROJECT MANAGER: AARON AMMON
COPY EDITOR: PAIGE TOWNLEY

GENERATE

CAMP by YM360

LEADING STUDENTS TO KNOW CHRIST & MAKE HIM KNOWN

GENERATESTUDENTS.COM

A 3-PART DEVOTIONAL EXPERIENCE
DESIGNED TO HELP YOU BECOME A DISCIPLE OF CHRIST. IN A WORD, TO KNOW GOD AND MAKE HIM KNOWN.

The *New/Next/Now* Discipleship Bundle provides three powerful devotional experiences to help you grow from a new believer to an authentic disciple of Christ.

NEW: FIRST STEPS FOR NEW CHRIST-FOLLOWERS

One of the most used new believer resources in youth ministry, this powerful 4-week devotional experience will help new believers get off to a strong start on their new journey with Christ.

NEXT: GROWING A FAITH THAT LASTS

4-week devotional will help you take ownership of your faith. NEXT will teach: Why it's important to own your faith, What life's purpose has to do with God's mission, How to build spiritual habits that last a lifetime, and How to use the influence you already have for Christ.

NOW: IMPACTING YOUR WORLD FOR CHRIST (RIGHT NOW!)

You have the amazing potential to impact your world for Christ, not just some time in the future ... but right NOW! Today. Your world is rich with opportunities to share the hopeful message of the Gospel, and to show people the amazing difference Christ can make in their lives. Now will help you make the most of these opportunities!

TO VIEW SAMPLES OF *NEW, NEXT & NOW* & TO ORDER, GO TO YM360.COM/DEVOBUNDLE

WHAT KEEPS YOU FROM BEING ALL THAT GOD HAS CALLED YOU TO BE?

Whatever it is, you need to know this: there is a better way. God wants you to face your fears and lean-in to who He desires you to be. If you're ready, Facing Your Fears is a great place to start.

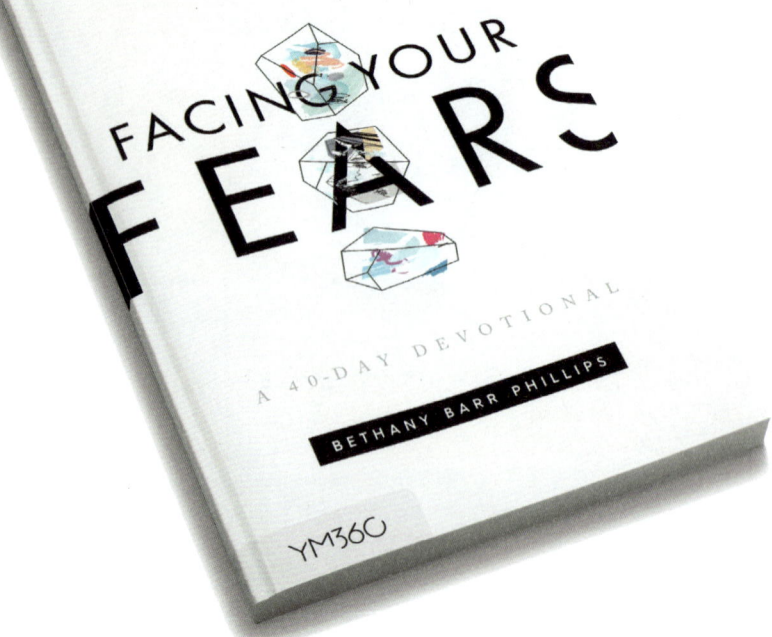

Facing Your Fears, a 40-day, Scripture-driven devotional by Bethany Barr Phillips, helps reveal where fear has taken hold of your life and equips you to put an end to these strongholds.

TO VIEW SAMPLES OF *FACING YOUR FEARS* & TO ORDER, GO TO YM360.COM/FEARS